CU00646541

© 2021 Victoria Careford-White. All rights reserved.
ISBN: 979-8-5848-0457-2
Imprint: Independently published.

This book belongs to

□□□ □□□ □□□ □□□ □□□ □□□ □□□ □□□ □□□ □□□ □□□ □□□ □□□ □□□ □□

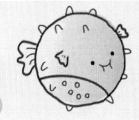

Guidance for Parents

This book is ideal for children aged 4 – 6 (Reception and Year 1 in England and Wales, Year 1 and Year 2 in Northern Ireland and Nursery, P1 and P2 in Scotland) to help with their understanding of number bonds. Being able to recall number bonds quickly is a huge help when it comes to mentally adding and subtracting; children will be able to apply their knowledge to a wide range of mathematical problems.

Understanding number bonds is one of the objectives of the Year 1 Maths Programme of Study (in England). The National Curriculum requirement is to: "represent and use number bonds and related subtraction facts within 20" (Department for Education, 2013). For Reception, the new Early Learning Goals for Number require children to: "have a deep understanding of number to 10, including the composition of each number; automatically recall... number bonds up to 5... and some number bonds to 10..." (Department for Education, 2020).

The main focus of this book is to learn and consolidate number bonds *of* 10 and 20, although the activities in the second part of the book also include number bonds *within* 20.

Having taught primary school children for over 16 years, I have designed this book to reflect how I have found children learn best and this is partly by repetition. The repetitive nature of the exercises in the first part are to ensure children have time to understand the process and fully implement what they have learnt. Working in 'order' also helps children to recognise patterns. Understanding patterns and working out 'rules' at an early age has been found to increase children's mathematical achievements later on in their schooling (Rittle-Johnson et al, 2016).

Using this Book

This book has been designed so that most children will be able to work independently once they have been shown how to complete one or two of the exercises. Some children will need more support than others. If you find your child is struggling, then grab some building blocks, cars or any other small objects and recreate the sums more visually.

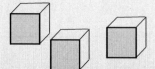
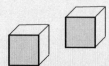

What are Number Bonds?

Number bonds are pairs of numbers that make another number. For example, 9 and 1 is a number bond of 10. 15 and 5 is a number bond of 20. 4 and 4 is a number bond of 8.

There are a number of ways to work out these pairs and different ways they can be represented. These are shown below.

Number Lines

Number lines are a visual way to help add and subtract. In this example, we are working out 9 + 1. Start at 9, jump on 1, land on 10.

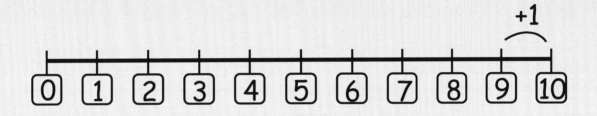

Tens Frames

A tens frame is a grid of 10. They can be filled with two differently-coloured counters for example, to show combinations to make 10. Two frames would be used to show 20.

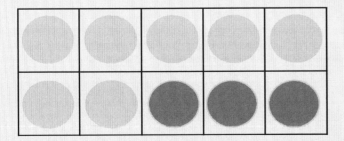

This shows that 7 and 3 make 10.

Other Ways to Show Number Bonds

- Number bonds can be shown in other ways, such as a part-whole method. These are simple diagrams that show how a number, such as 10, can be split into two other numbers, such as 6 and 4 or 8 and 2.

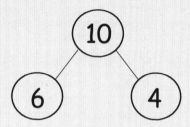

- Multilink or blocks can also be used to show representations visually. Use two different colours to show each number.

- Numicon is also a great resource. These are flat shapes with holes, each hole representing one number, so the number three is a flat, plastic shape with three holes. This will fit together with the shape representing seven, to make a grid of ten.

- Make it real. Putting candles on a cake – if there are 5, how many more do you need to add if the birthday child is 9 years old?

- Use dominoes to pair numbers. Can your child find two dominoes that, put together, make 5?

  Or they can add up the numbers on a single domino. So, for the domino shown below, 1 + 3 = 4:

Number Sentences

Number sentences are statements like 5 + 5 = 10, 17 + 3 = 20 or 10 – 2 = 8. Children are often asked to fill in the missing number, for example 7 + ? = 10 or ? + 1 = 20.

Cut out these number lines to help you on some of the activities in the second half of this book.

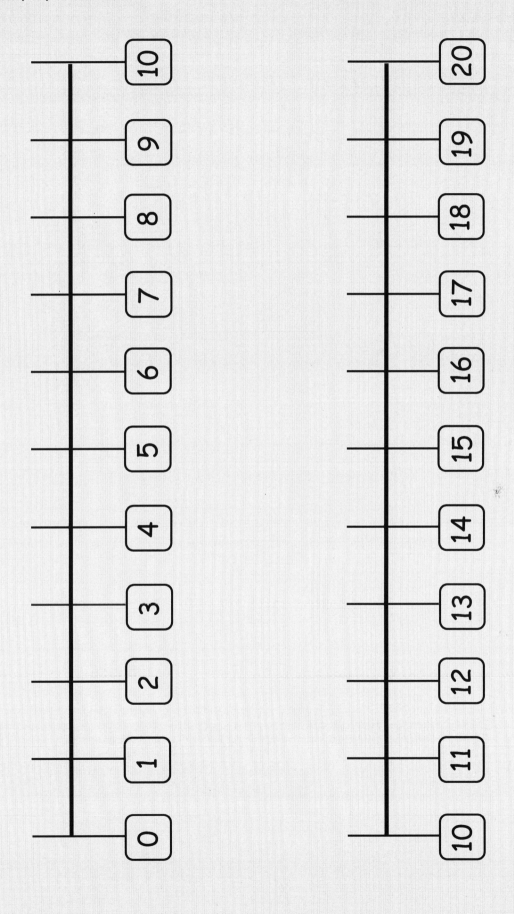

Blank page

Contents

The first four sections are the repetitive part of the book, which, as mentioned, is important for understanding. These sections focus on number bonds of 10 and 20.

From section 5 onwards, activities are more varied and from section 6, include different number bonds within 20.

1. **Number bonds of 10** Draw the missing sea creature or ocean object into the tens frame, colour them in and complete the sum. This section includes both combinations of bonds of 10, e.g. 7 + 3 and 3 + 7.

2. **Number bonds of 20** Same as the first section, but for number bonds of 20.

3. **Number bonds of 10 - Draw your own!** In this section, children are learning to count to 10 by drawing their own sea creatures (or anything else they like).

4. **Number bonds of 20 - Draw your own!** Draw your own! Same as for the previous section, but counting to make bonds of 20.

5. **Tens frames** Draw the missing pictures into the tens frames and complete the sums with answers of 10 or 20. These are not in order.

6. **Number bonds within 20** Children complete the diagrams to make bonds within 20.

7. **Bond matching** Draw lines to match the bonds for answers within 20.

8. **Bond pairs** Fill in the missing numbers to make various number bonds.

9. **Number sentences** Fill in the missing numbers.

10. **Under the sea activities** Various activities to practise all numbers bonds within 20.

11. **Number bond game** Cut out and play this game where you have to work out sums to move on to the finish.

12. **Colouring page**

7 + 3

6 + 4

Number

bonds

9 + 1

5 + 5

# of 10

8 + 2

10 + 0

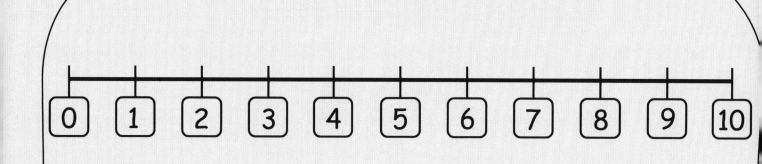

ten plus zero equals ten

+ = **10**

Nothing needs to go here...

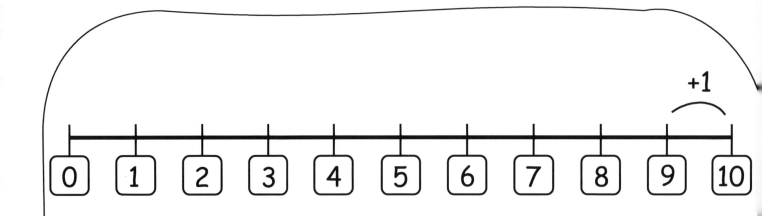

Draw the missing pufferfish to make 10.

nine plus one equals ten

$$9 + 1 = 10$$

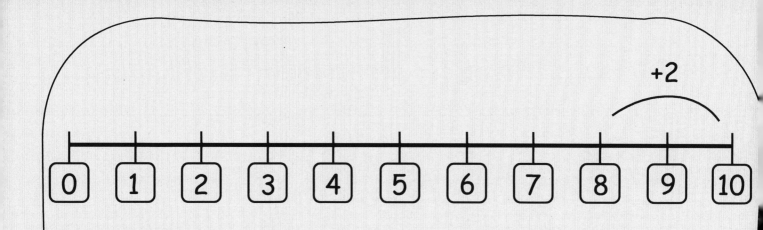

+2

0 1 2 3 4 5 6 7 8 9 10

Draw the missing starfish to make 10.

eight plus two equals ten

$\boxed{8} + \boxed{2} = 10$

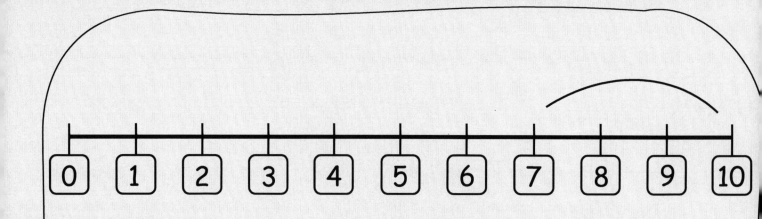

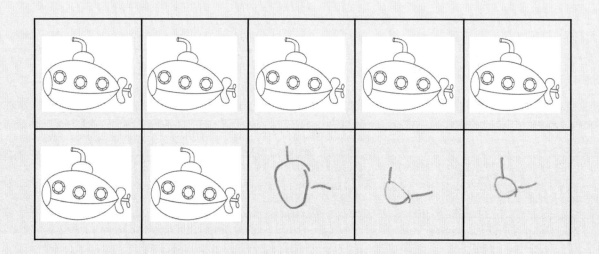

Draw the missing submarines to make 10.

seven plus three equals ten

$$\boxed{7} + \boxed{3} = 10$$

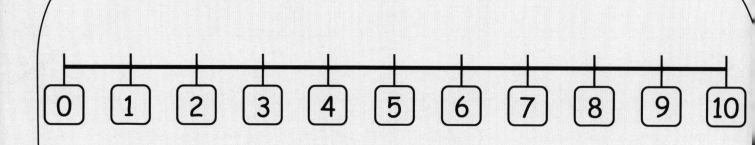

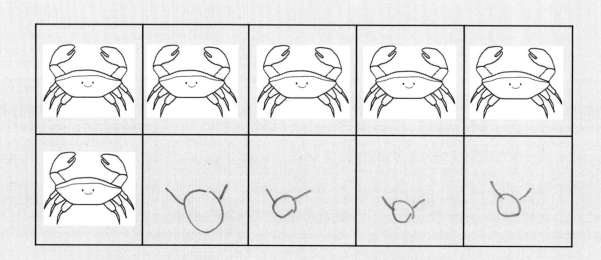

Draw the missing crabs to make 10.

six plus four equals ten

$$6 + 4 = 10$$

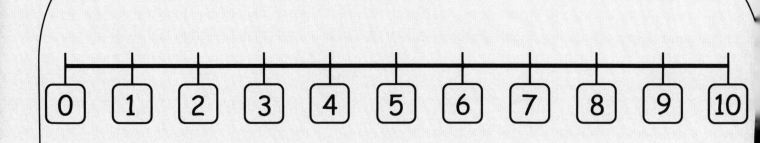

Draw the missing octopuses to make 10.

five plus five equals ten

$\boxed{} + \boxed{} = 10$

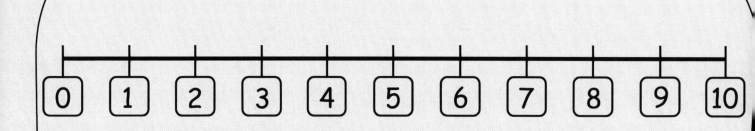

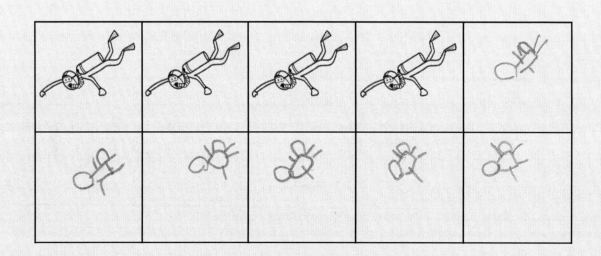

Draw the missing divers to make 10.

four plus six equals ten

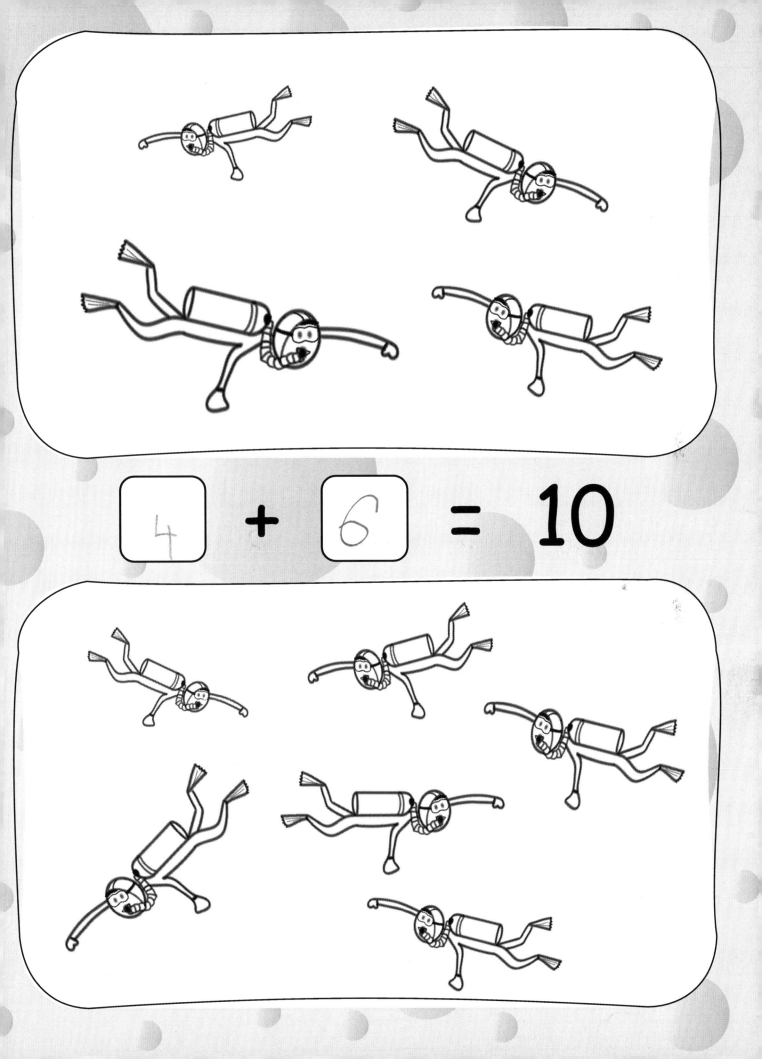

$$4 + 6 = 10$$

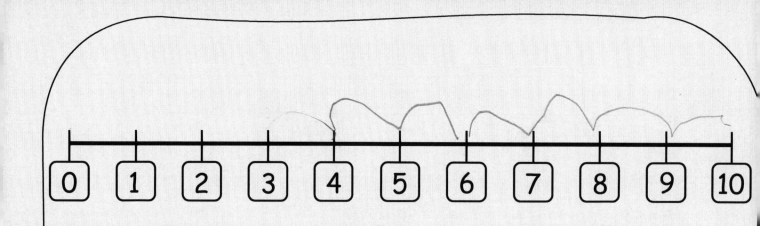

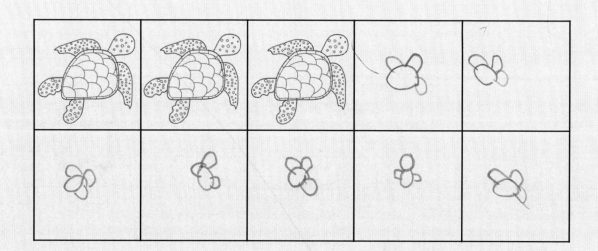

Draw the missing sea turtles to make 10.

three plus seven equals ten

$$\boxed{3} + \boxed{7} = \mathbf{10}$$

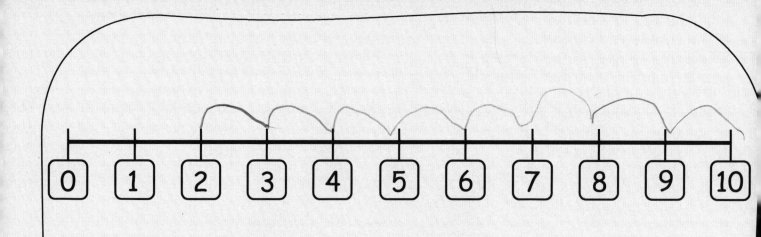

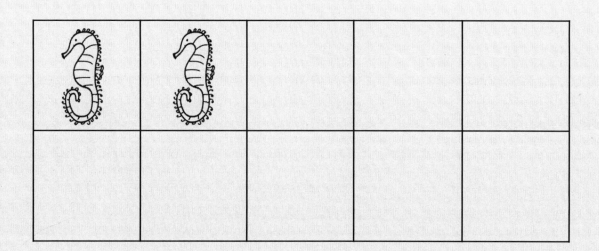

Draw the missing seahorses to make 10.

two plus eight equals ten

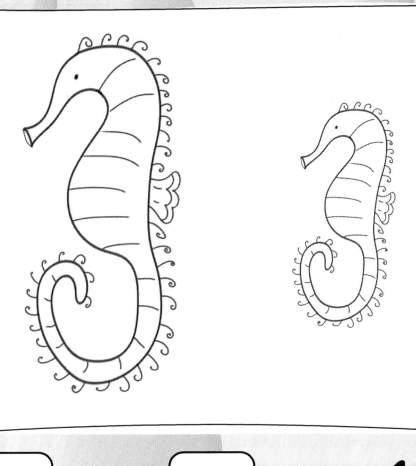

2 + 8 = 10

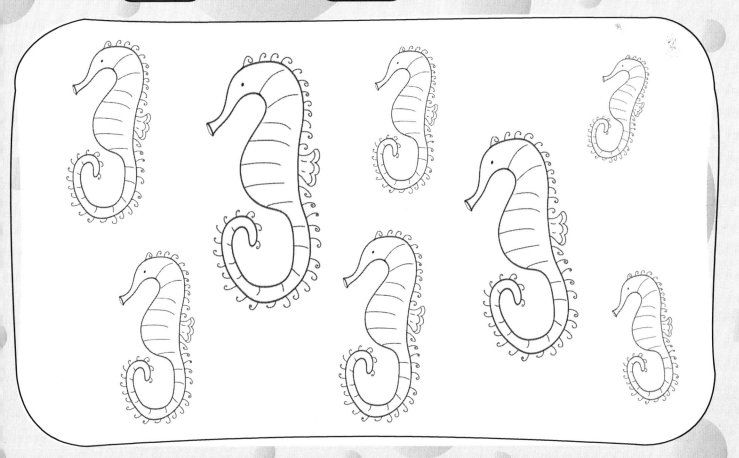

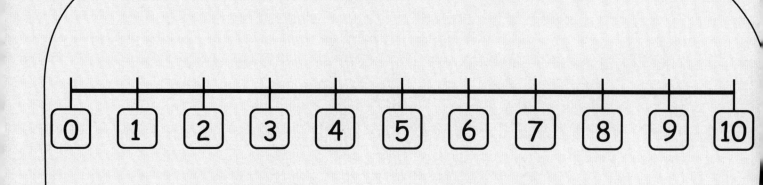

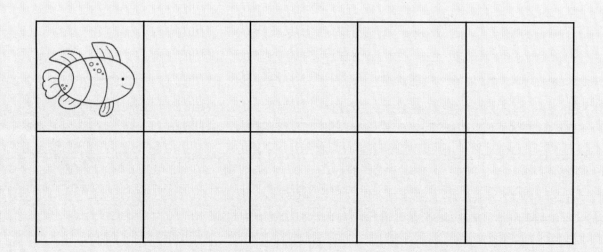

Draw the missing fish to make 10.

one plus nine equals ten

☐ + ☐ = 10

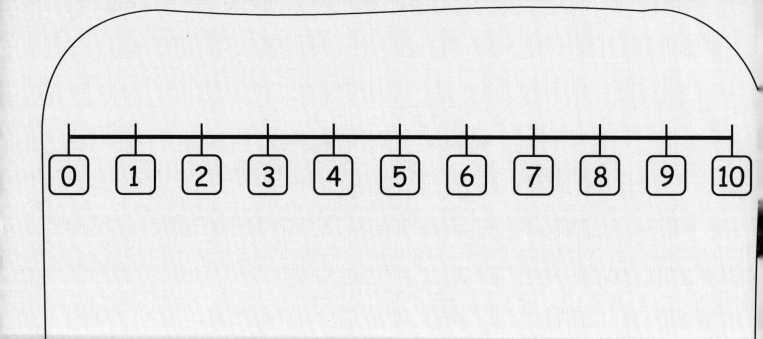

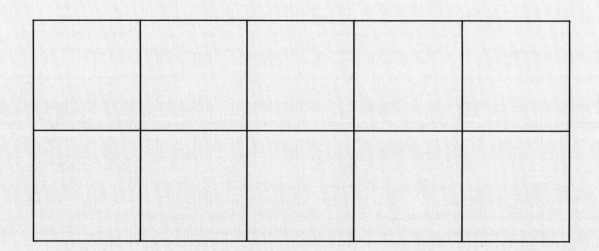

Draw the missing anchors to make 10.

zero plus ten equals ten

$\boxed{} + \boxed{} = 10$

15 + 5

13 + 7

Number

bonds

19 + 1

12 + 8

# of 20

10 + 10

11 + 9

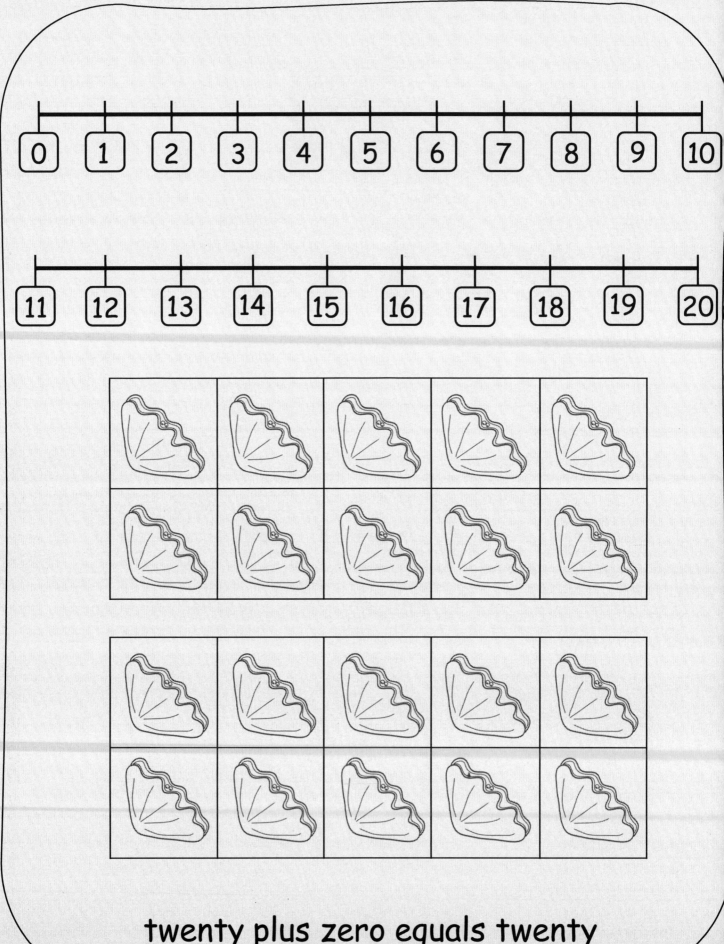

twenty plus zero equals twenty

| | + | | = 20

Nothing needs to go here...

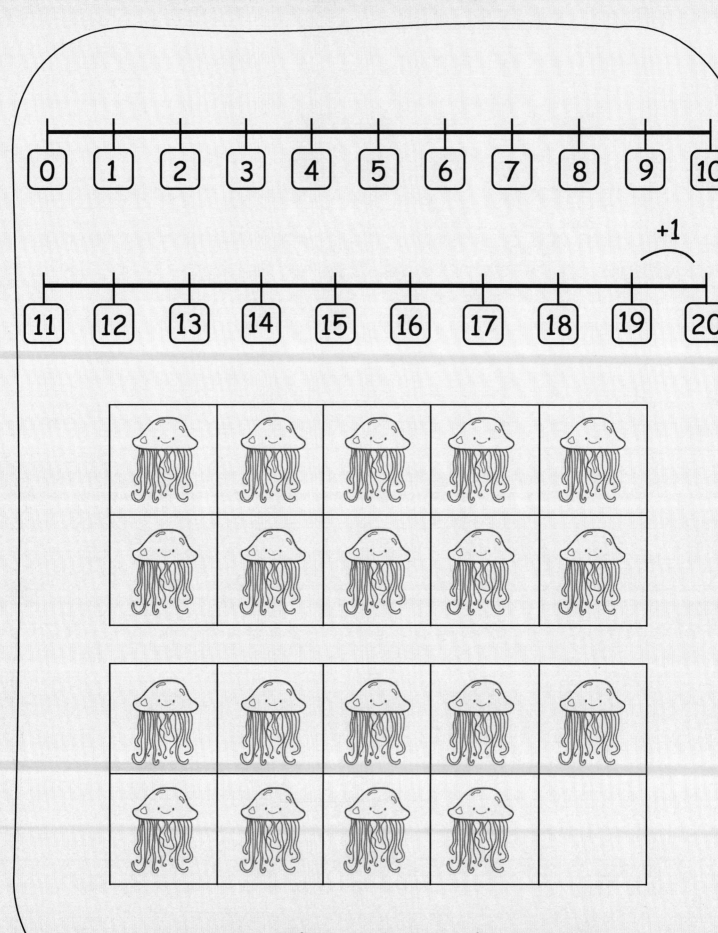

nineteen plus one equals twenty

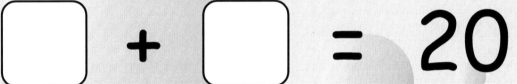

☐ + ☐ = 20

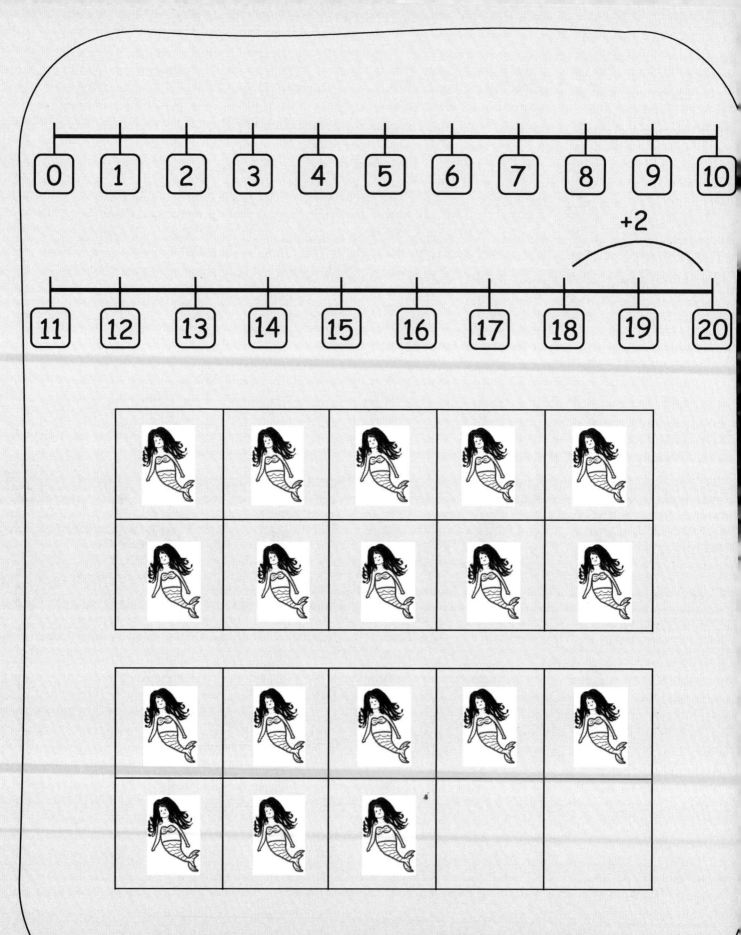

eighteen plus two equals twenty

$$\boxed{} + \boxed{} = 20$$

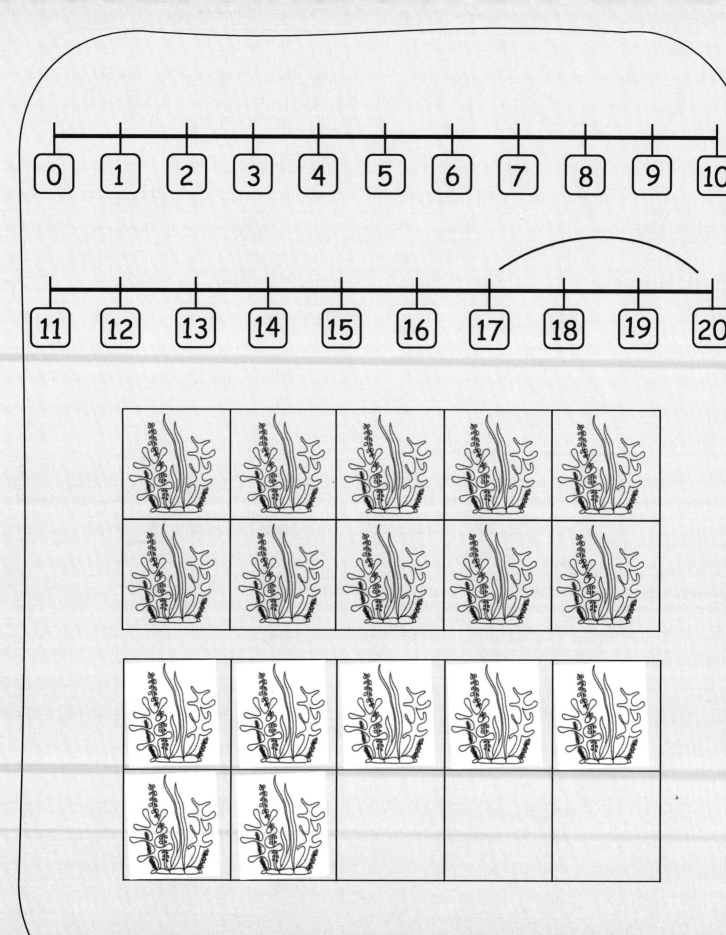

seventeen plus three equals twenty

$+$ $=$ 20

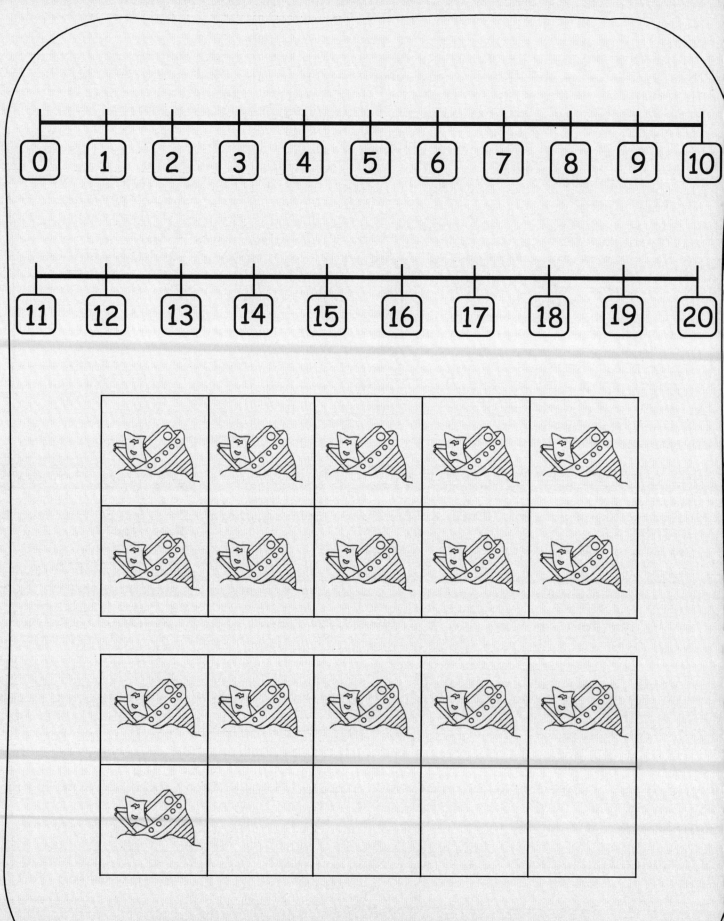

sixteen plus four equals twenty

$$\boxed{} + \boxed{} = 20$$

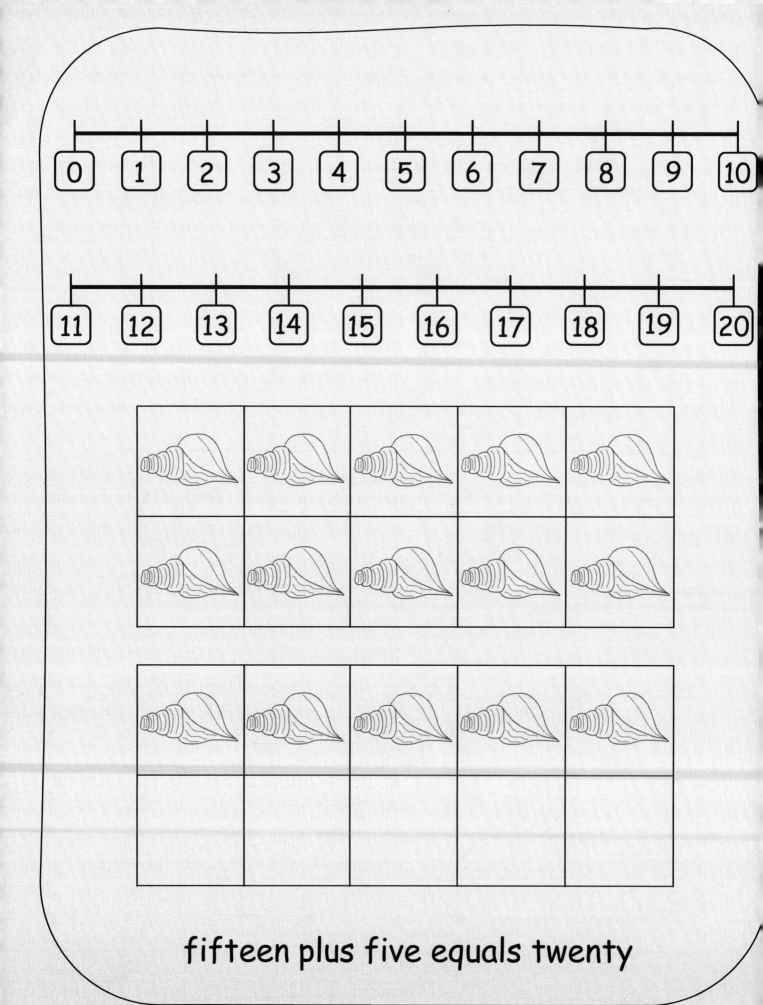

fifteen plus five equals twenty

+ = 20

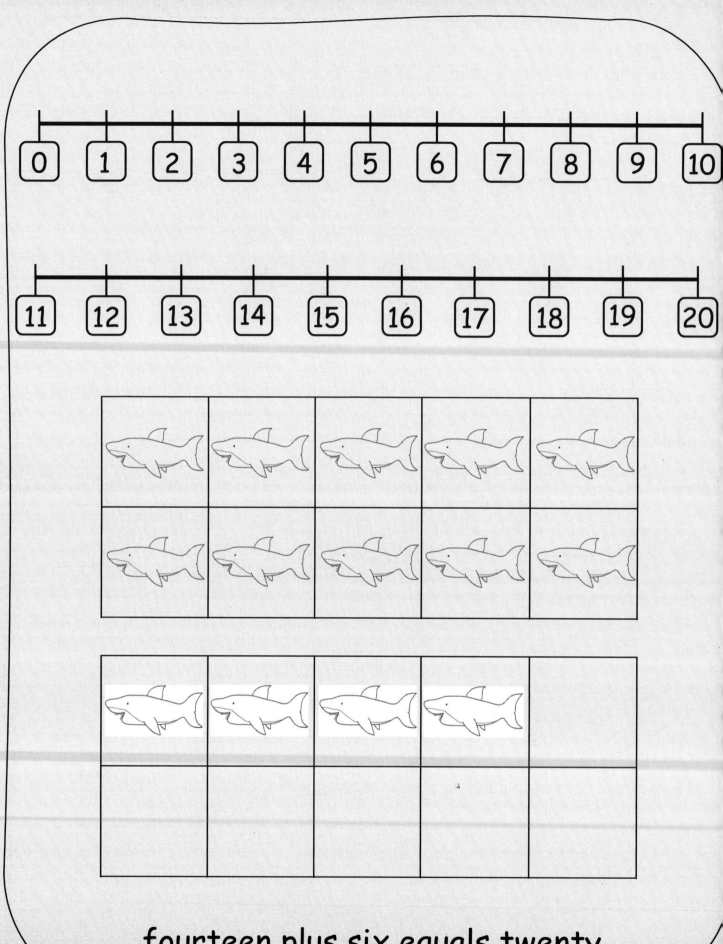

fourteen plus six equals twenty

☐ + ☐ = 20

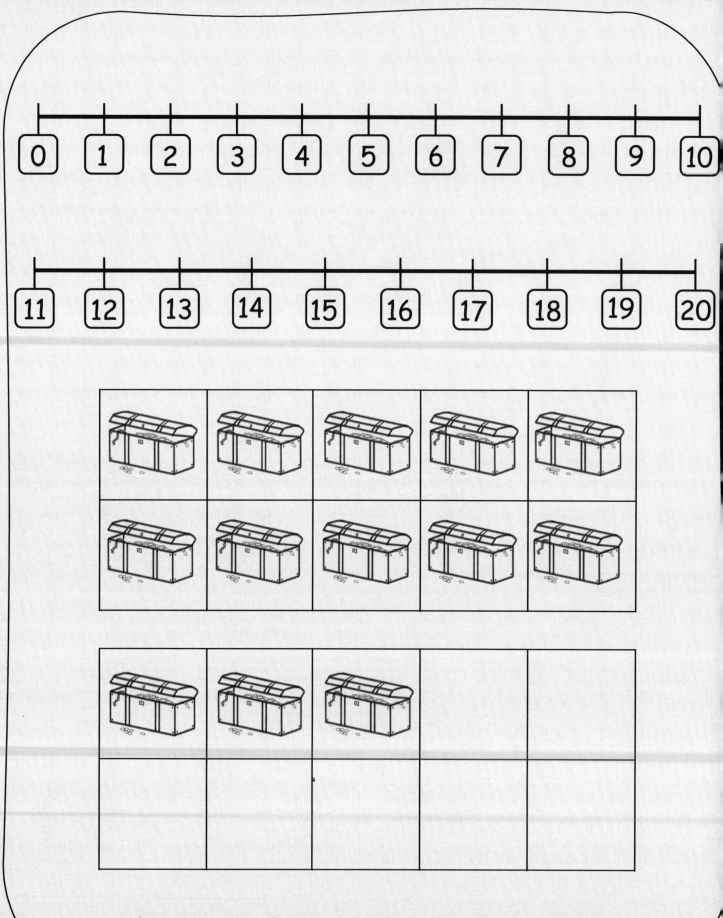

thirteen plus seven equals twenty

+ = 20

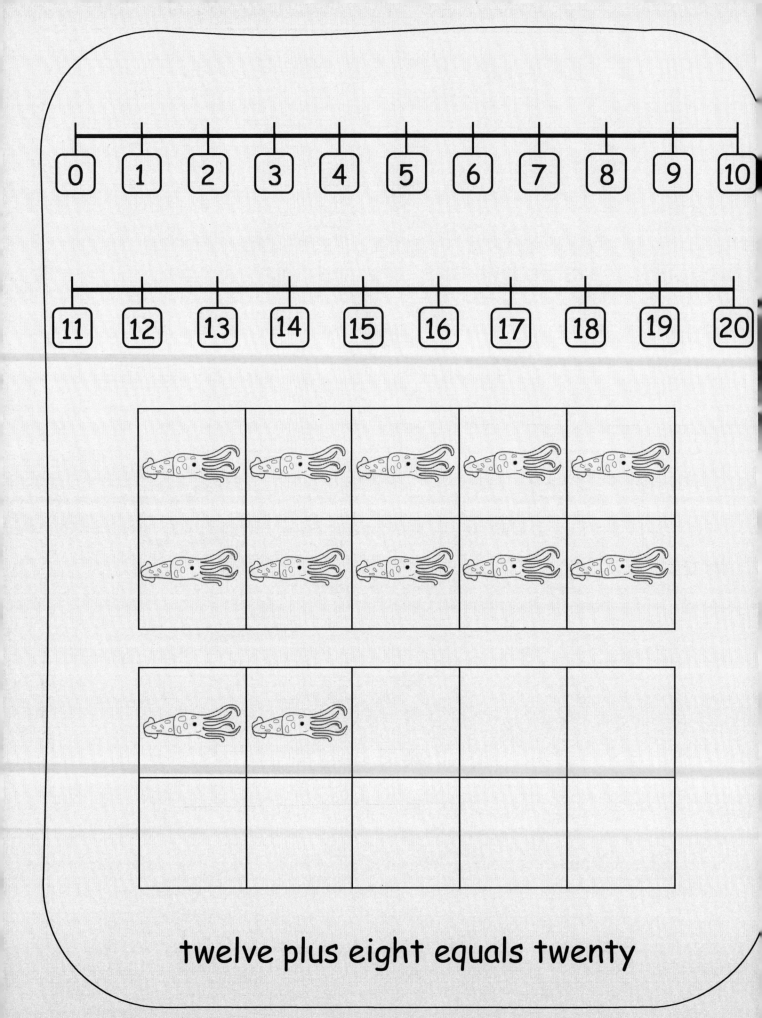

twelve plus eight equals twenty

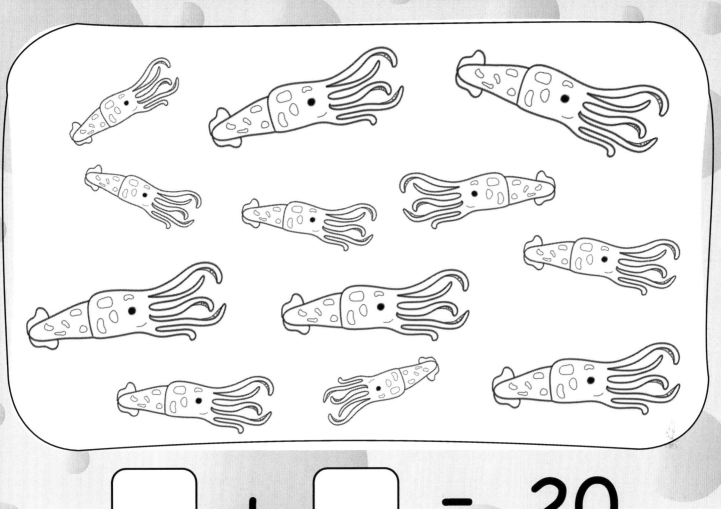

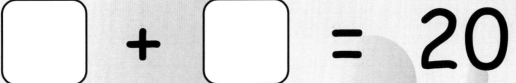

+ = 20

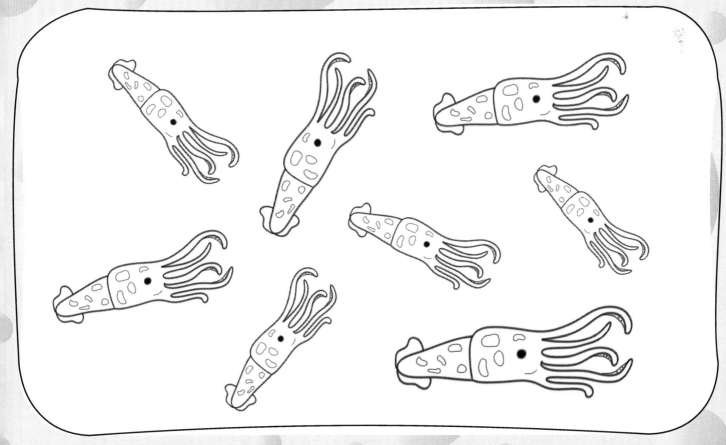

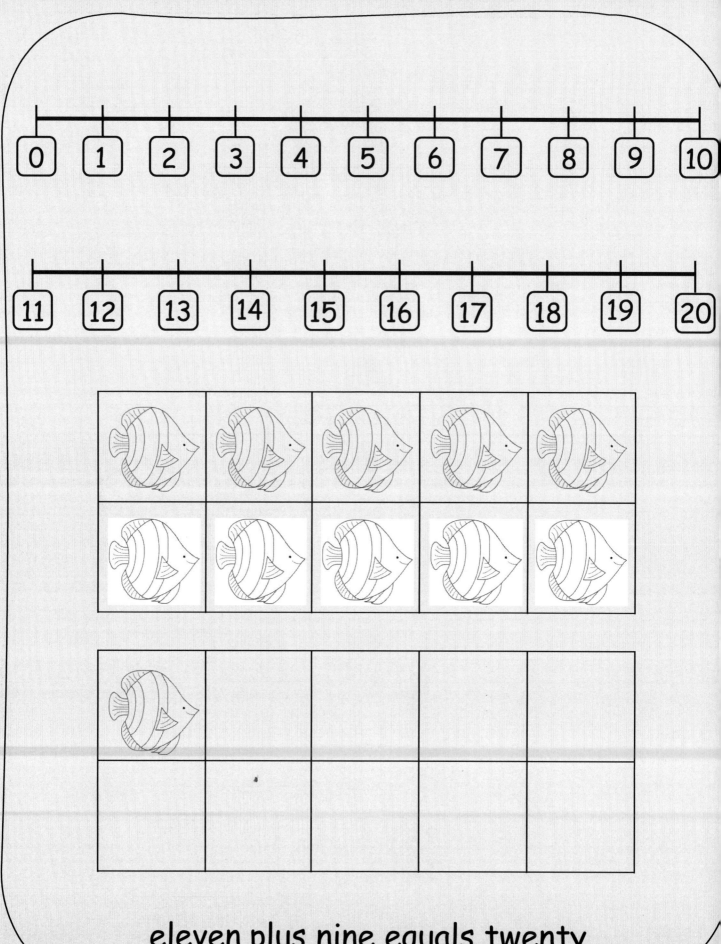

eleven plus nine equals twenty

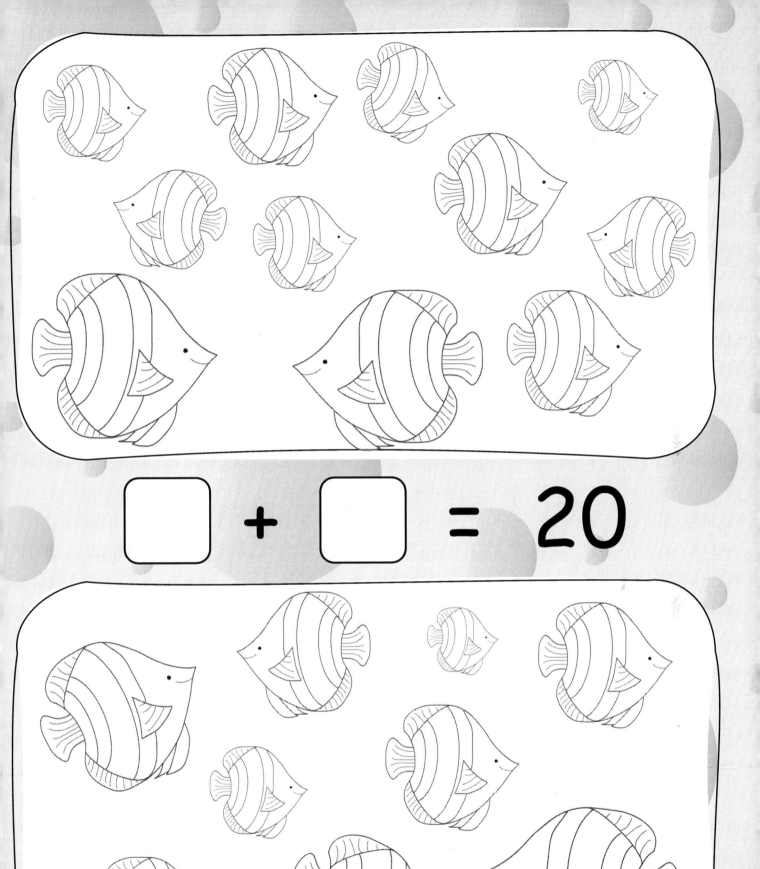

$\boxed{}$ **+** $\boxed{}$ **= 20**

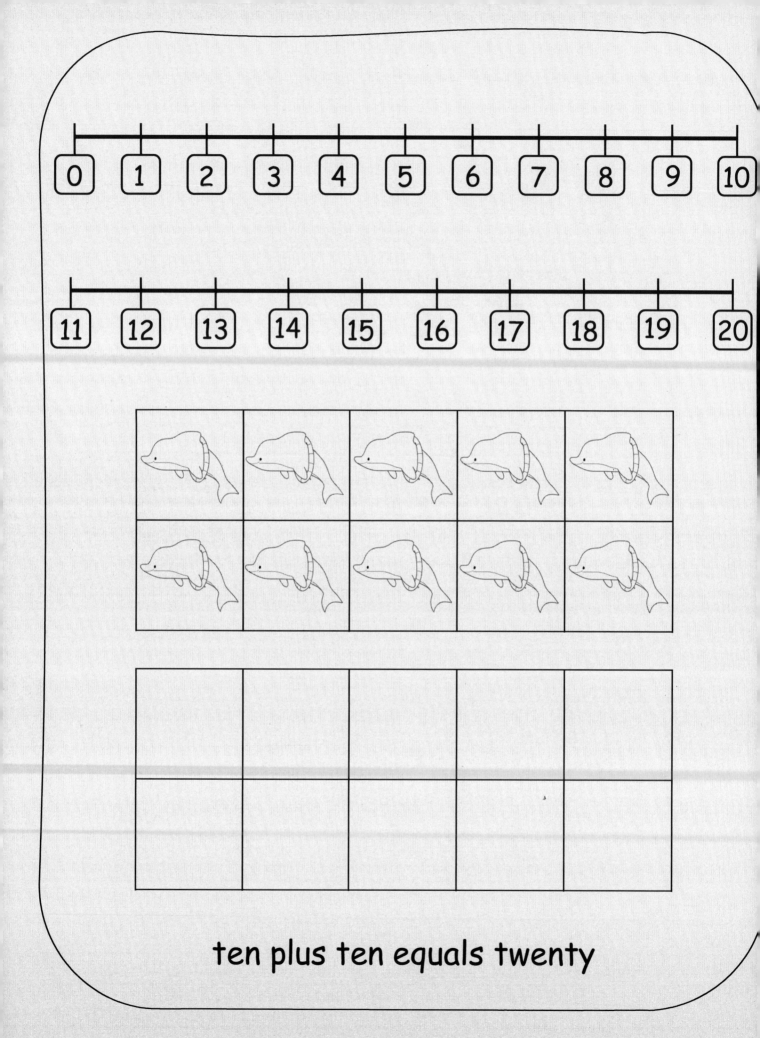

ten plus ten equals twenty

☐ + ☐ = 20

Number bonds of 10

Draw your own!

Draw 10 of something here...

10 + 0 = 10

No need to draw anything here...

9 + 1 = 10

$$8 + 2 = 10$$

7 + 3 = 10

6 + 4 = 10

5 + 5 = 10

4 + 6 = 10

3 + 7 = 10

2 + 8 = 10

1 + 9 = 10

0 + 10 = 10

Number bonds of 20

Draw your own!

20 + 0 = 20

$$19 + 1 = 20$$

18 + 2 = 20

17 + 3 = 20

16 + 4 = 20

15 + 5 = 20

$$14 + 6 = 20$$

13 + 7 = 20

12 + 8 = 20

11 + 9 = 20

10 + 10 = 20

Tens frames

Draw the missing pictures, colour in two different colours and finish the sums.

$7 \;+\; \boxed{3} \;=\; 10$

$6 \;+\; \boxed{4} \;=\; 10$

$5 \;+\; \boxed{5} \;=\; 10$

$8 \;+\; \boxed{2} \;=\; 10$

$14 + \boxed{6} = 20$

$17 + \boxed{3} = 20$

$18 + \boxed{2} = 20$

Number bonds within 20

Draw the missing sea creatures.

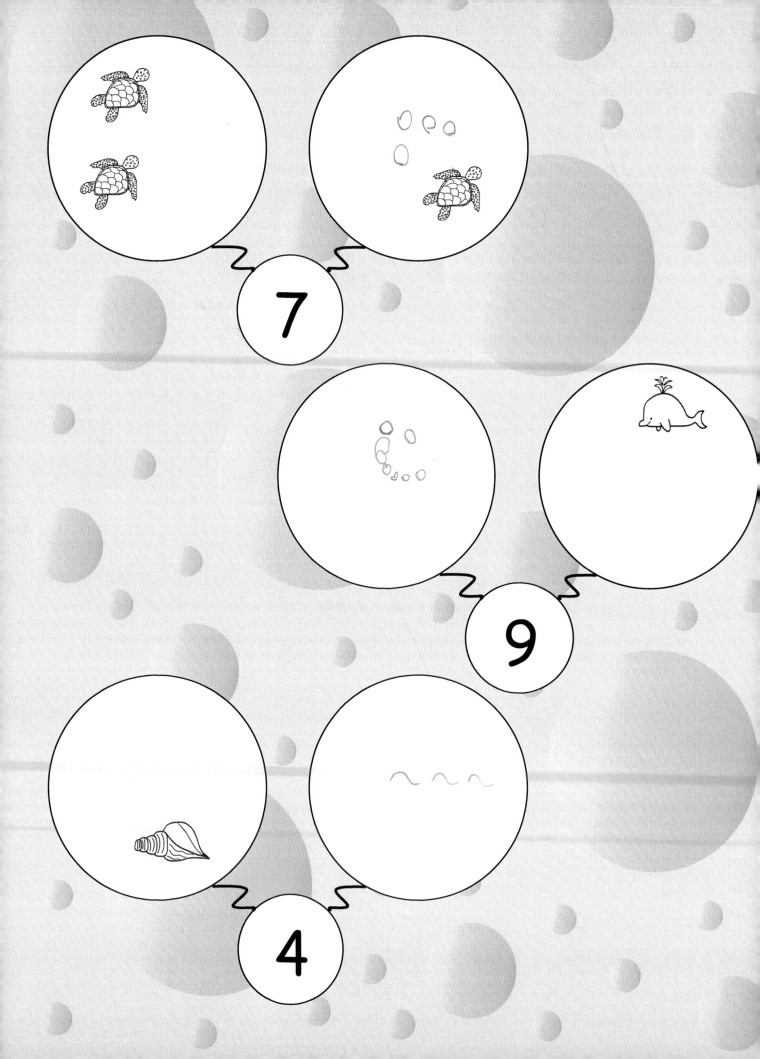

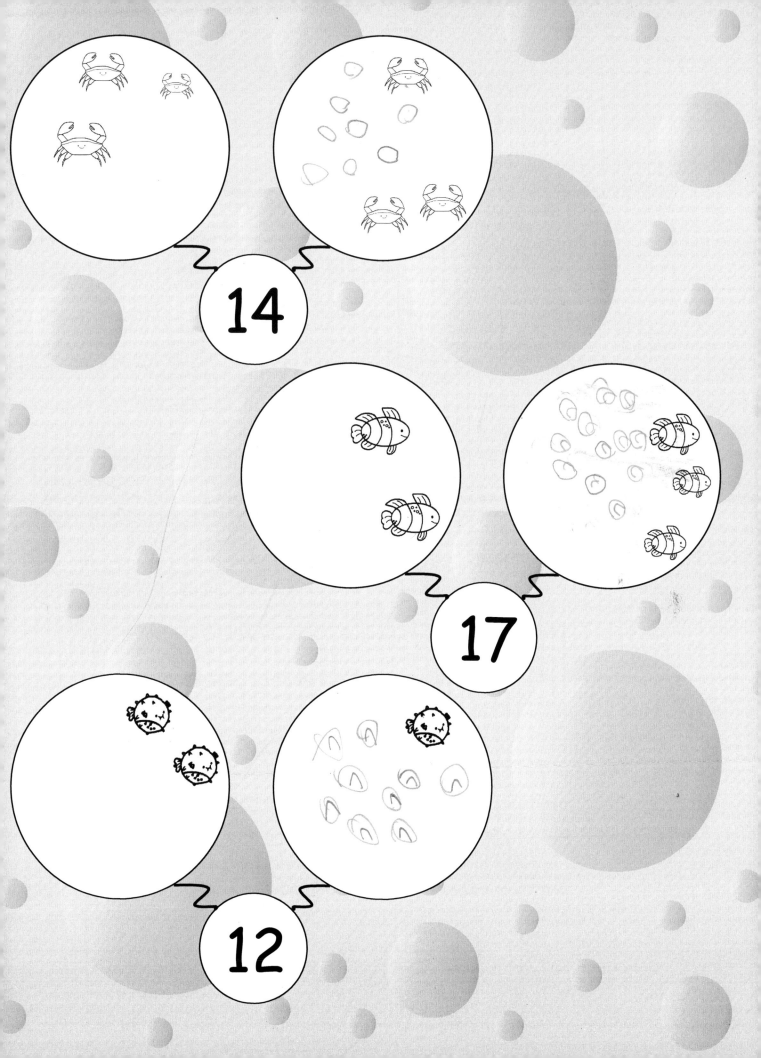

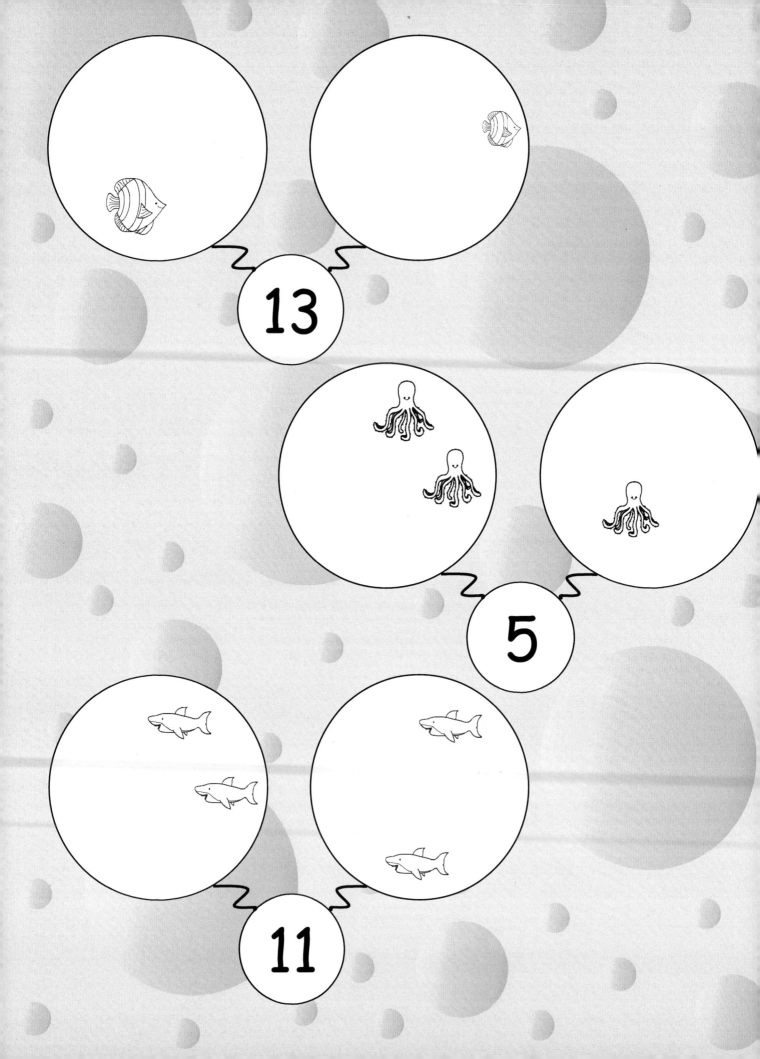

Bond matching

Draw lines to match the number bonds.

Draw lines to pair number bonds of 10.

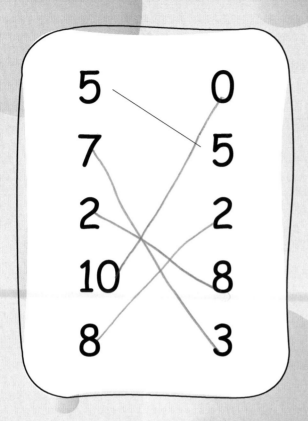

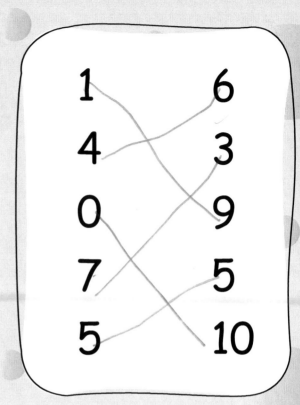

Draw lines to pair number bonds of 20.

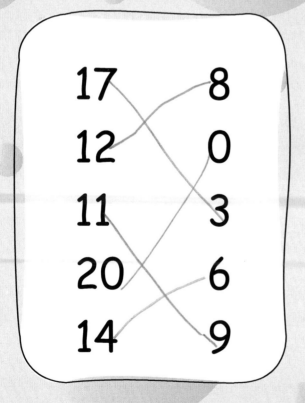

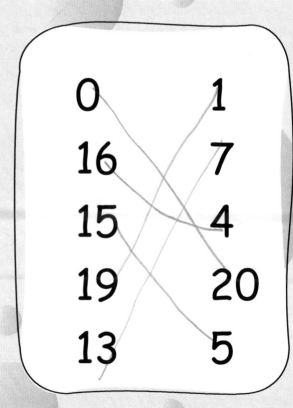

Draw lines to pair number bonds of 8.

5	8
0	4
3	1
4	3
7	5

Draw lines to pair number bonds of 6.

4	0
2	2
6	1
5	3
3	4

Draw lines to pair number bonds of 7.

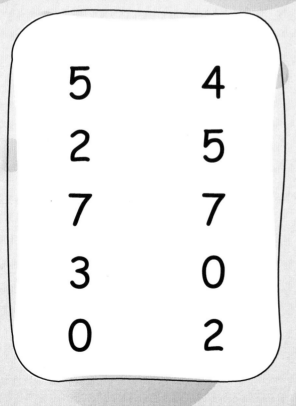

5	4
2	5
7	7
3	0
0	2

Draw lines to pair number bonds of 9.

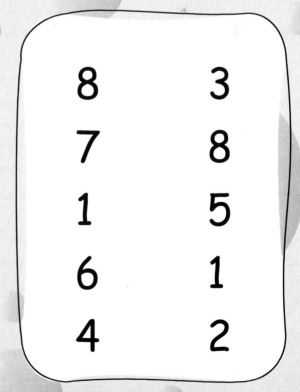

8	3
7	8
1	5
6	1
4	2

Draw lines to pair number bonds of 13.

10	5
8	3
9	1
12	7
6	4

Draw lines to pair number bonds of 11.

7	0
9	2
11	3
8	4
1	10

Draw lines to pair number bonds of 19.

15	2
17	16
3	6
11	8
13	4

Draw lines to pair number bonds of 15

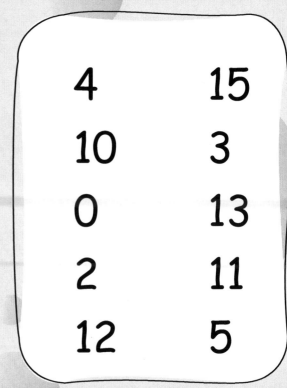

4	15
10	3
0	13
2	11
12	5

Bond pairs

Fill in the missing numbers.

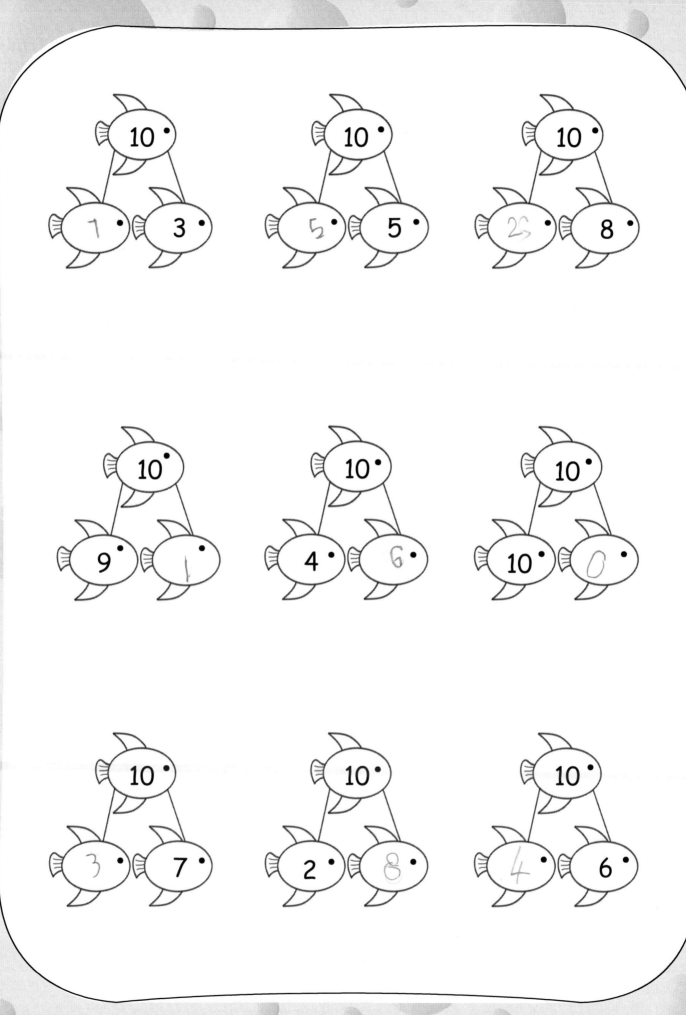

USING A NUMBER LINE

USING A NUMBER LINE

Number sentences

Fill in the missing numbers.

| 0 | 1 | 2 | 3 | 4 | 5 | 6 | 7 | 8 | 9 | 10 |

$5 + \boxed{} = 10$ $8 + \boxed{} = 10$

$3 + \boxed{} = 10$ $9 + \boxed{} = 10$

$6 + \boxed{} = 10$ $2 + \boxed{} = 10$

$\boxed{} + 1 = 10$ $\boxed{} + 7 = 10$

$\boxed{} + 4 = 10$ $\boxed{} + 10 = 10$

$\boxed{} + 6 = 10$ $\boxed{} + 3 = 10$

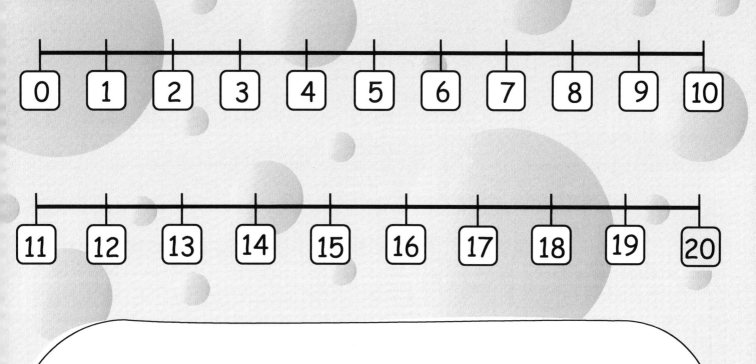

$17 + \boxed{} = 20$ $12 + \boxed{} = 20$

$14 + \boxed{} = 20$ $11 + \boxed{} = 20$

$16 + \boxed{} = 20$ $13 + \boxed{} = 20$

$\boxed{} + 7 = 20$ $\boxed{} + 5 = 20$

$\boxed{} + 4 = 20$ $\boxed{} + 2 = 20$

| 0 | 1 | 2 | 3 | 4 | 5 | 6 | 7 | 8 | 9 | 10 |

$3 + \boxed{} = 7$ $2 + \boxed{} = 5$

$9 + \boxed{} = 9$ $4 + \boxed{} = 8$

$7 + \boxed{} = 8$ $6 + \boxed{} = 9$

$\boxed{} + 4 = 5$ $\boxed{} + 2 = 7$

$\boxed{} + 3 = 6$ $\boxed{} + 1 = 2$

$4 + 2 = \boxed{}$ $5 + 3 = \boxed{}$

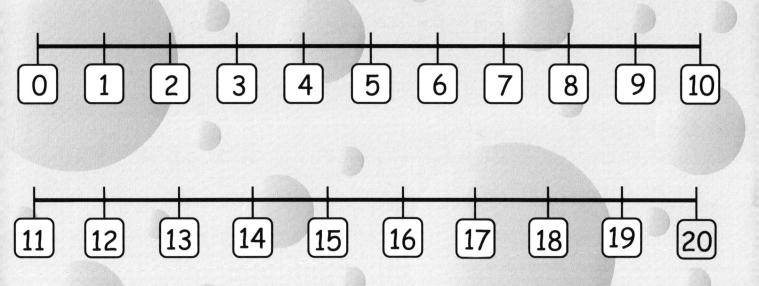

$11 + \boxed{} = 15$ $16 + \boxed{} = 18$

$13 + \boxed{} = 17$ $11 + \boxed{} = 19$

$12 + 5 = \boxed{}$ $18 + 0 = \boxed{}$

$\boxed{} + 5 = 12$ $\boxed{} + 3 = 19$

$\boxed{} + 4 = 11$ $\boxed{} + 9 = 17$

Under the sea

Number bond

activities

Diver Dan has found a sunken treasure chest with lots of gold coins!
He is playing a matching game with Maisie Mermaid.

Which coin should Maisie Mermaid match with Diver Dan's two coins?

Mrs Pufferfish has asked her class to find a partner to make 10.
Can you circle the partners?

The windows on the submarine have steamed up! Can you work out the missing numbers and write them into the foggy windows?

Jellicoe Jellyfish and Oscar Octopus want to play Tentacle Tangle! Colour the tentacles to make number bonds of 20. Use a different colour for each pair.

Write pairs of numbers on the seaweed pods to make the big number at the top.

Colour the pairs that make 2 in yellow, 3 in orange, 4 in brown, 5 in blue, 6 in red, 7 in pink, 8 in green, 9 in purple and 10 in grey.

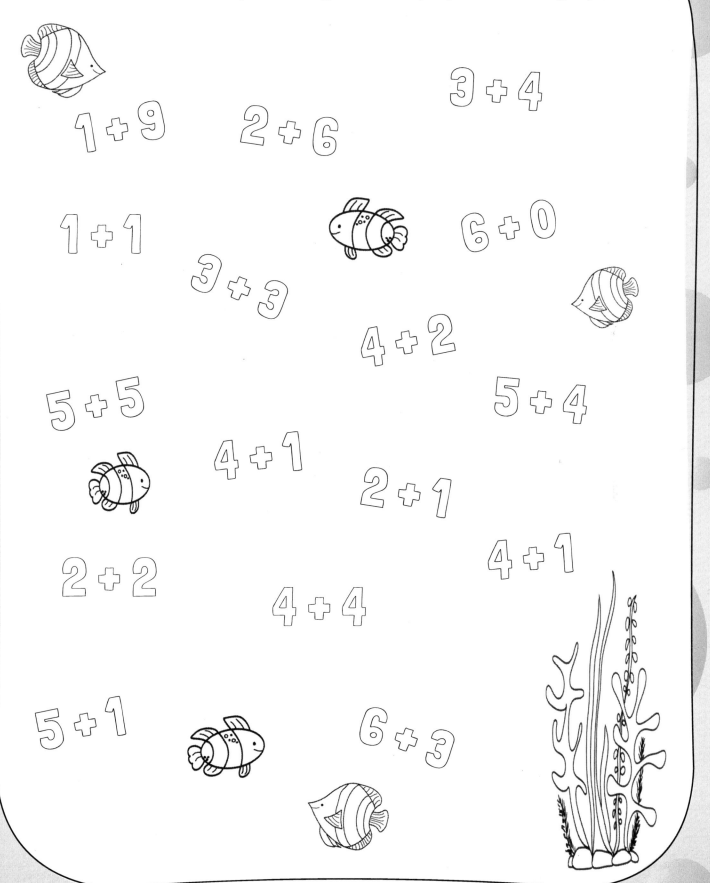

Some of the sea creatures are playing hook-an-anchor! They need to pick an anchor that makes **20**. Can you colour all the anchors with number bonds of **20**?

Shelley Shark loves popping bubbles! She also loves the number 20! Draw lines to make pairs of 20 to help Shelley pop her favourite number.

10

5

4

13

19

12

8

10

15

7

11

1

20

16

14

6

9

2

17

0

3

18

Sidney Starfish is playing hide and seek with his friends! They are safe if they match the numbers on the rocks. Can you help?

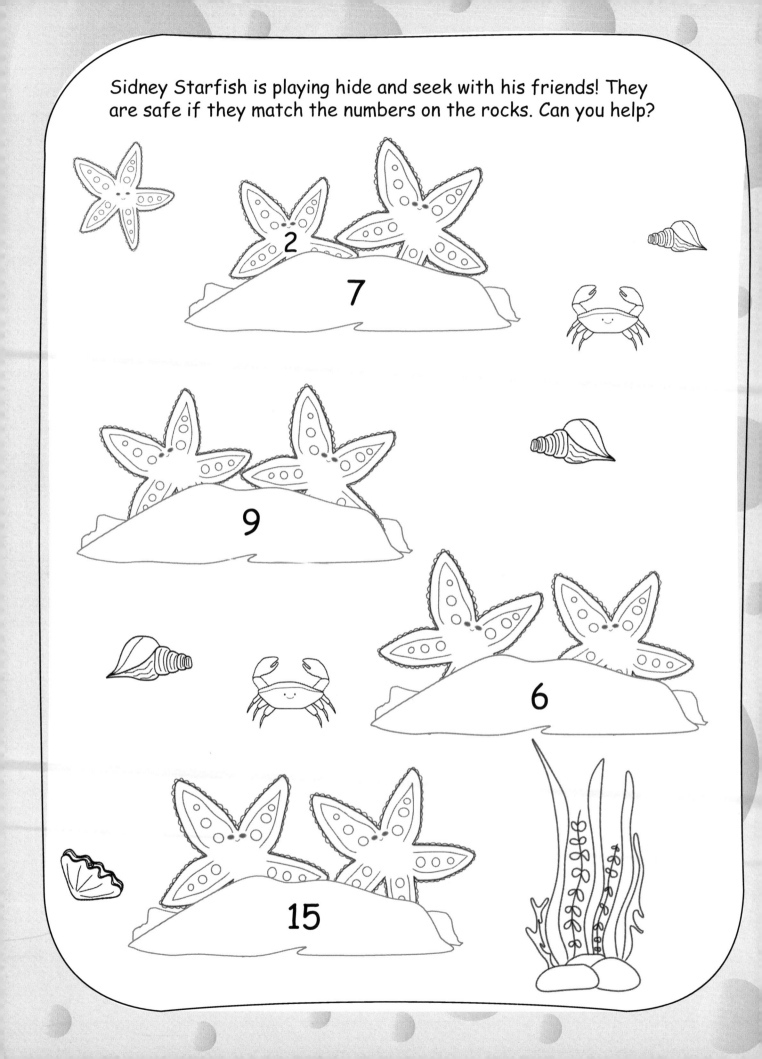

Make up your own number bond game! Think of all the ways you can show pairs of numbers. Which sea creatures will be in your game?

Under the sea

Number bond game

Number Bond Game! Ask an adult to cut out this page and the next. You could stick them on some cardboard to make them stronger. You will need a dice and some counters.

Start

6+3

5+1

8+2

2+1

7+2

Miss a go

3+0

4+3

4+4

1+1

7+0

2+4

9+1

0+5

Extra go

3+2

6+3

3+1

6+2

Roll the dice, move on the number rolled, work out the sum and move on that number. Your turn then ends. The winner is the first to the finish!

Finish

0+1

2+0

3+1

2+3

5+2

Miss a go

1+4

6+1

4+0

Shortcut swim!

3+3

7+1

5+4

4+1

6+0

8+1

Blank page

Under the sea Colouring

Blank page

References

Department for Education (2013, September). *Mathematics programmes of study: Key stages 1 and 2 national curriculum in England.* Retrieved from: https://assets.publishing.service.gov.uk/government/uploads/system/uploads/attachment_data/file/335158/PRIMARY_national_curriculum_-_Mathematics_220714.pdf

Department for Education (2020, July). *Statutory framework for the early years foundation stage: Setting the standards for learning, development and care for children from birth to five - EYFS reforms early adopter version.* Retrieved from: https://assets.publishing.service.gov.uk/government/uploads/system/uploads/attachment_data/file/896810/EYFS_Early_Adopter_Framework.pdf

Rittle-Johnson, B., Fyfe, E. R., Hofer, K. G., & Farran, D. C. (2016). Early math trajectories: Low-income children's mathematics knowledge from ages 4 to 11. *Child Development, 88*(5), 1727-1742. https://srcd.onlinelibrary.wiley.com/doi/abs/10.1111/cdev.12662

Printed in Great Britain
by Amazon

56110943R00072